Great Rivers

Rivers of the United Kingdom

Catherine Brereton

 raintree

a Capstone company — publishers for children

Raintree is an imprint of Capstone Global Library Limited, a company incorporated in England and Wales having its registered office at 264 Banbury Road, Oxford, OX2 7DY – Registered company number 6695582

www.raintree.co.uk
myorders@raintree.co.uk

Text © Capstone Global Library Limited 2018
The moral rights of the proprietor have been asserted.

Produced by Brown Bear Books Ltd:
Text: Catherine Brereton
Design Manager: Keith Davis
Editorial Director: Lindsey Lowe
Children's Publisher: Anne O'Daly
Picture Manager: Sophie Mortimer

ISBN: 978 1 4747 5400 2
21 20 19 18 17
10 9 8 7 6 5 3 2 1

British Library Cataloguing-in-Publication Data
A full catalogue record for this book is available from the British Library.

Acknowledgements
We would like to thank the following for permission to reproduce photographs:
123rf: Peter Titmuss, 15; Alamy: Acorn 5, 22, Commission Air, 7, Epicscotland, 25, Heather Drake, 21, i4images rm, 9, Mike Howitt, 23, Powered by Light/Alan Spencer, 8; Braintree Canoeing Club: 14; iStock: 1, 28 (centre left), CaronB, 5 (top), George-Standen, 11, John F. Scott, 28 (right), Jolanda Aalbers, 5 (bottom), MikeLane45, 13; Public Domain: FT magazine, 19; Roger Keech Productions Ltd: 27; Shutterstock: Helen Hotson, 4-5, IR Stone, 18, Madrugada Verde, cover, Martin Prochazkacz, 26, Maziarz, 17; Thinkstock: iStock, 28 (bottom)

Brown Bear Books has made every attempt to contact copyright holders of material reproduced in this book. Any omissions will be rectified in subsequent printings if notice is given to the publisher. If anyone has any information please contact licensing@brownbearbooks.co.uk

Contents

Some words are shown in bold, **like this**. You can find out what they mean by looking in the glossary.

What are rivers?

Rivers are channels of fresh water flowing through the landscape. The start of a river is called its **source**. The river flows from its source downhill towards the sea.

A river grows bigger as it travels towards the sea. Small rivers and **streams** join together and form bigger rivers. Rivers bring water to the land so that plants can grow. People use rivers and water in lots of ways. The United Kingdom has many important rivers.

This river is flowing fast as it travels downhill from its source.

Many towns were originally built next to rivers. Rivers provided transportation and drinking water.

Wye Bridge, across the River Wye, Hereford

Golitha Falls, Cornwall

Rivers are home to many types of birds, insects, fish and other animals.

The Avon

The River Avon begins at a **spring** in central England. There are ten British rivers called Avon. This one is sometimes called the Warwickshire Avon or the Upper Avon.

Where:
Central England

How long: 154 km (96 miles)

Main towns/cities: Rugby, Warwick, Stratford-upon-Avon, Evesham, Tewkesbury

The Avon is also a **tributary** of the River Severn. It joins the Severn at Tewkesbury.

Rugby

Warwick

Stratford-upon-Avon

Evesham

Tewkesbury

— River Severn

Bristol Channel

The river gets wider and deeper as it flows along.

As it goes along, the River Avon shapes the landscape. It flows along in big curves called meanders. The river flows through a **valley**. The Avon valley is famous for its stunning scenery.

Rivers and **canals** were once important for transporting goods. **Locks** were built to raise or lower boats where stretches of the river or canal were at different levels. Now the boats on the River Avon are mainly for fun.

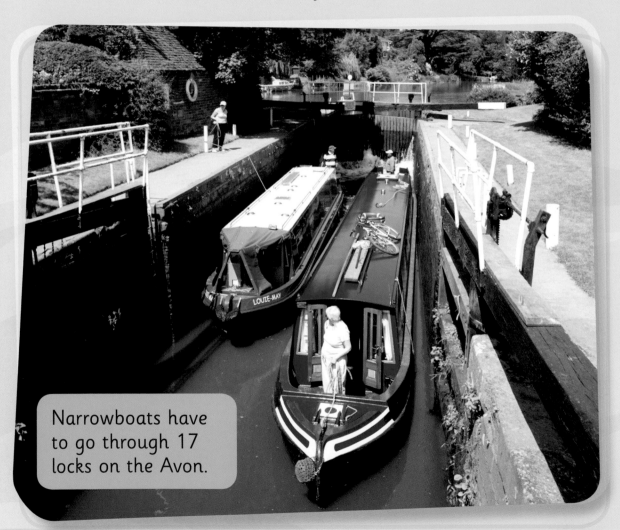

Narrowboats have to go through 17 locks on the Avon.

Boats gather each year to celebrate the river festival in Stratford-upon-Avon.

One of Britain's most famous writers, William Shakespeare, was born in Stratford-upon-Avon. The town is popular with tourists. Many people visit the town to see Shakespeare's plays performed at The Royal Shakespeare Theatre next to the river.

The Mersey

The River Mersey begins in the Pennine Hills. It becomes a wide **estuary** before it meets the sea in Liverpool Bay. **Ferries** have taken people across the Mersey estuary since **medieval** times.

The Mersey was once very dirty. It has been cleaned up and wildlife, such as otters and even seals, now live there again.

Where: North-west England

How long: 110 km (70 miles)

Main towns/cities: Stockport, Warrington, Birkenhead, Liverpool

Irish Sea

Liverpool

Birkenhead

Warrington

Stockport

The old Albert Dock in Liverpool is now a tourist attraction. Museums tell the story of the city's past.

Liverpool is a busy **port**. Until the mid-1900s ships carried sugar, cotton, timber and grain all over the world. Today, Liverpool is an important port for huge container ships.

The Severn

The River Severn is the longest river in the United Kingdom. It starts at the top of the Cambrian Mountains in Wales. The river flows down through Wales and England to the Bristol Channel.

The **estuary** of the River Severn is over 8 km (5 miles) wide.

Where: Wales and West of England

How long: 354 km (220 miles)

Main towns/cities: Newtown, Welshpool, Shrewsbury, Ironbridge, Worcester, Gloucester

Welshpool

Shrewsbury

Ironbridge

Newtown

Worcester

Tewkesbury

Gloucester

Bristol channel

This brightly-coloured kingfisher dives into the water of the River Severn to catch a fish.

Rivers are important **habitats** for animals. Fish, frogs, newts and snails live in rivers. The River Severn is home to many animals. Dragonflies flutter above the water. Birds hunt for food in the river and nest on its banks.

In some rivers, the **tide** coming in from the sea travels all the way up the river. This is called a tidal bore. The River Severn has one of the largest tidal bores in the world! There are 260 tidal bores on the Severn each year.

A tidal bore makes waves as high as 3 metres (10 feet).

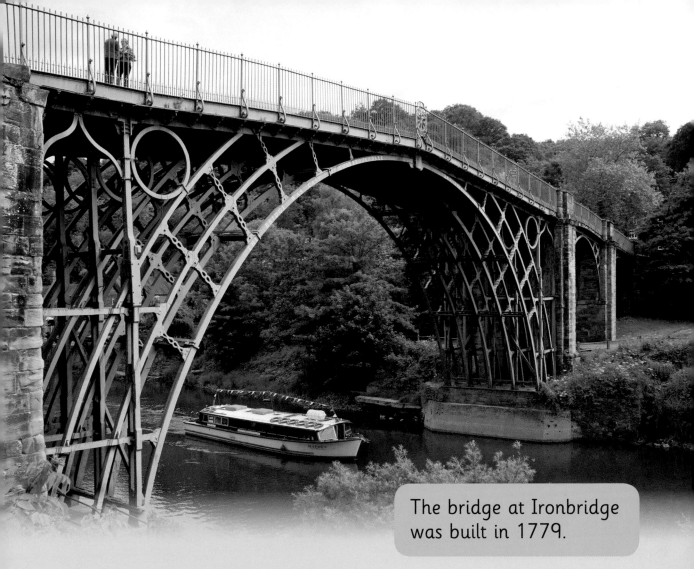

The bridge at Ironbridge was built in 1779.

The **Industrial Revolution** started in the Severn **valley** in the 1770s. Abraham Darby invented a new way to make iron and built the world's first cast-iron bridge. The bridge spans the River Severn.

The Thames

London is the **capital city** of the United Kingdom. The River Thames flows through central London. More than eight million people live in London. Some people use river buses and taxis to get to and from work.

Two thirds of London's drinking water comes from the River Thames.

Where:
South-east England

How long: 330 km (205 miles)

Main towns/cities:
Oxford, Reading, Henley, Marlow, Windsor, Teddington, London, Southend-on-Sea

Tower Bridge is London's most famous bridge across the Thames.

The River Thames flows east from a small **stream** in the Cotswold Hills. It opens into a wide **estuary** at Southend-on-Sea. A footpath, the Thames Path National Trail, starts in the Cotswold Hills. It ends at the Thames Barrier in Greenwich, London.

If there is a storm or a very high **tide**, London is at risk of being flooded. The Thames Barrier protects the city. If there is going to be a high tide, the gates are shut to keep the water out.

The Thames Barrier has ten huge steel gates across the river.

The Thames froze solid for two months in 1683–1684. Londoners set up camps selling food and drink.

Between 1600 and 1814 winter frost fairs were held on the River Thames. The water froze solid. Winters are warmer now. The river no longer freezes but people still have fun on the Thames. Today, they enjoy water sports such as rowing and kayaking.

The Trent

The River Trent is the third-longest river in the United Kingdom. Its **source** is at Biddulph Moor in Staffordshire. It flows from there through the Midlands and into the Humber **estuary**.

Where: Central England

How long: 270 km (168 miles)

Main towns/cities: Stoke-on-Trent, Burton-upon-Trent, Nottingham, Newark

The River Trent flows northwards, which is unusual for rivers in Britain.

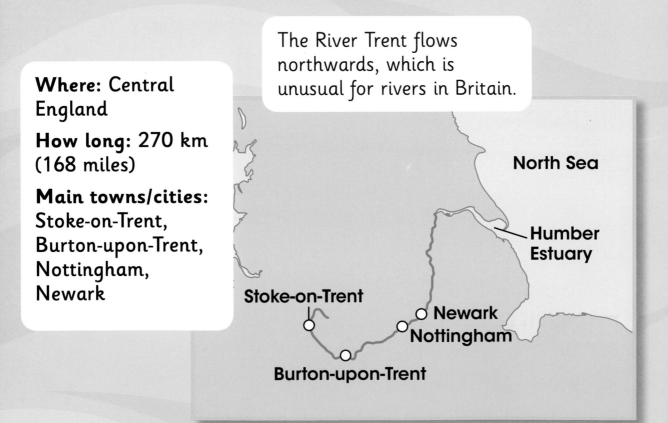

North Sea

Humber Estuary

Stoke-on-Trent

Newark
Nottingham

Burton-upon-Trent

Trent Bridge in Nottingham is one of the Trent's most famous landmarks.

Nottingham first had a bridge and a busy market in **medieval** times. The town grew quickly as the river became an important route for transport and **trade**.

Fast-flowing water from rivers creates energy. People can use the energy to drive **turbines** in machines called **generators**. These machines create electricity.

Beeston Weir is one of many small power stations along the River Trent.

Rubbish in the River Trent is one type of pollution. It can harm wildlife.

Pollution is a problem in many rivers. Harmful chemicals from factories and farms sometimes spill into rivers. Sewage can also be a problem. Pollution kills fish and other wildlife. It is also dangerous for people. It is important to keep rivers clean.

The Tweed

The River Tweed starts as a tiny **burn** at Tweed's Well, high in the Scottish mountains. The river journeys through southern Scotland. It crosses the border into England and flows into the North Sea.

For 27 km (17 miles) the River Tweed forms the border between Scotland and England.

Where: Scotland and North of England

How long: 156 km (97 miles)

Main towns/cities: Peebles, Galashiels, Kelso, Berwick-upon-Tweed

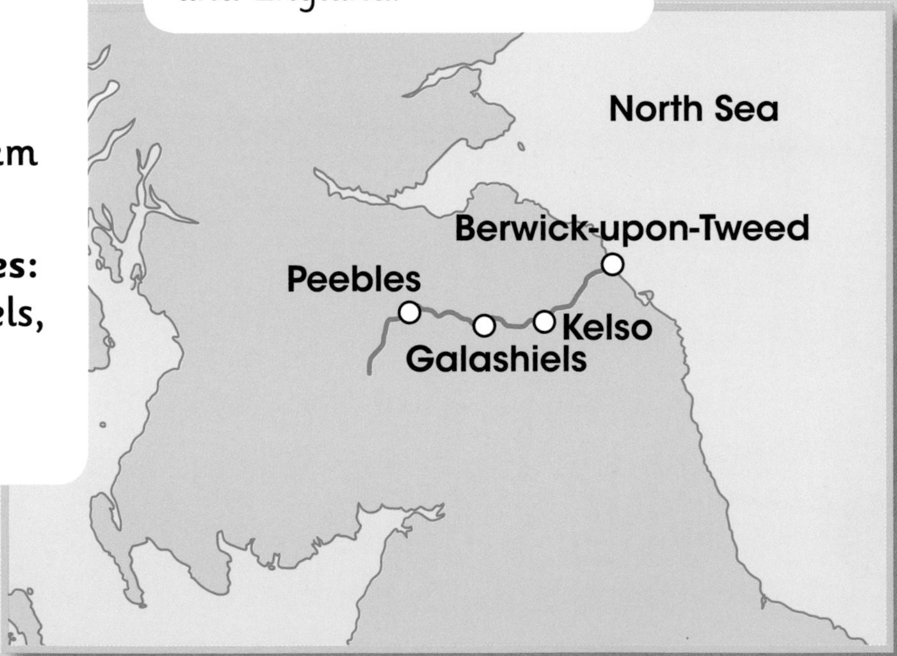

North Sea

Berwick-upon-Tweed

Peebles

Kelso

Galashiels

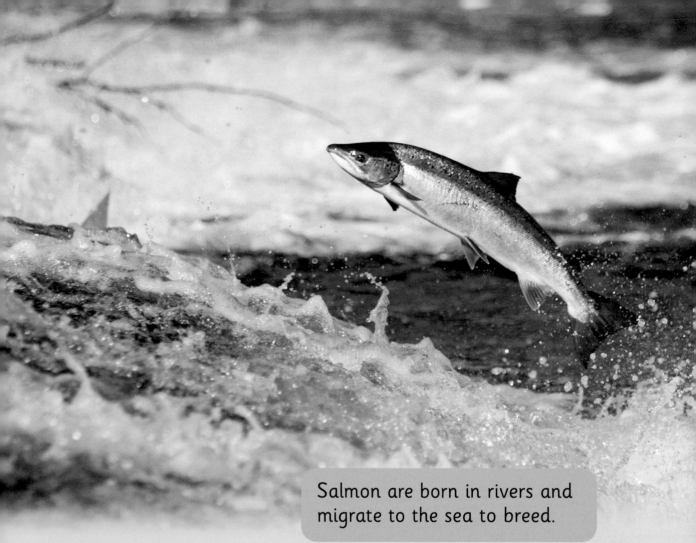

Salmon are born in rivers and migrate to the sea to breed.

The Tweed is famous for its salmon. The clean, cold waters make it an ideal **habitat** for these fish. Many people visit the Tweed to go salmon fishing. They also visit the area to spot the rare osprey. Ospreys are birds of prey that feed on salmon.

A hundred years ago, ospreys had disappeared from Britain. They were killed by **pesticides** used on farms, and people stole their eggs. Conservation projects gradually helped ospreys return to Scotland. Today several pairs of ospreys nest in the Tweed **valley** every year.

This osprey has plucked a fish out of the River Tweed.

The River Tweed meets the sea at the border town of Berwick-upon-Tweed.

From the 1100s to the 1400s, the border between Scotland and England was moved several times. Berwick-upon-Tweed was sometimes in Scotland and sometimes in England! Today it is England's most northerly town.

Other UK rivers

The River Wye flows along the border of Wales and England. Wildlife includes bats and the rare polecat!

The River Clyde was important for shipbuilding in the 1900s. Shipbuilding was once a major industry in **Glasgow**.

The Great Ouse hosted the Oxford and Cambridge boat race in 1944. This is the only time the race has not been held on the Thames.

The River Bann is the longest river in Northern Ireland. It flows into Lough Neagh, which is the largest lake in the United Kingdom.

The Clifton Suspension Bridge crosses the Bristol Avon's dramatic cliffs and **gorge**.

The River Tyne flows into the North Sea after a journey of 100 km (62 miles) across northern England. The city of Newcastle upon Tyne is famous for its swing bridge.

Location of rivers

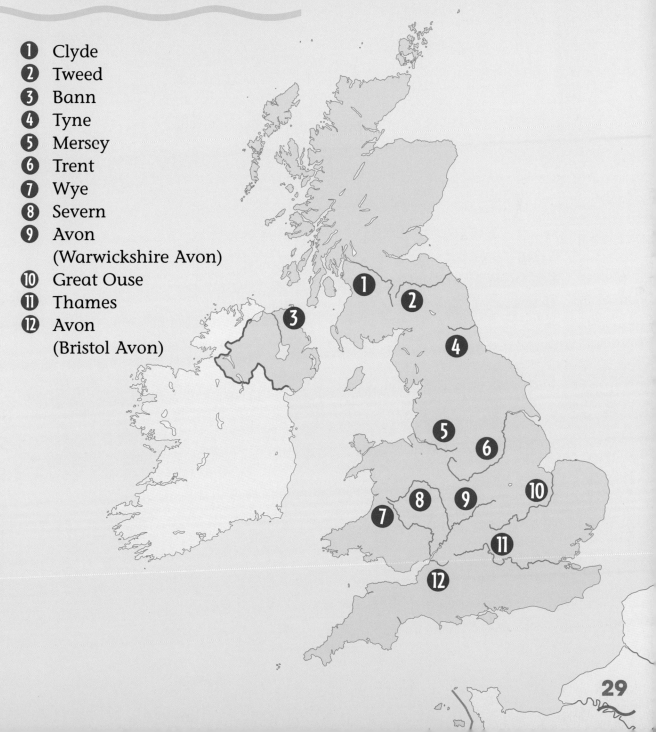

1 Clyde
2 Tweed
3 Bann
4 Tyne
5 Mersey
6 Trent
7 Wye
8 Severn
9 Avon
   (Warwickshire Avon)
10 Great Ouse
11 Thames
12 Avon
   (Bristol Avon)

Glossary

burn Scottish word for a stream

canal human-made waterway linking rivers

capital city the main city of a country

estuary the mouth of a large river where it meets the sea

ferry a small boat or ship that takes passengers across a river

generator a machine that produces electricity

gorge a deep, narrow valley with steep, rocky sides

habitat the place where an animal or plant lives

Industrial Revolution a period in history when many factories were built and people moved from the countryside to work in towns and cities

lock an enclosed chamber on a river or canal, with gates at either end, to raise or lower boats from one water level to another

medieval a period in history, sometimes known as the Middle Ages, from around 500 to 1500 CE.

pollution anything that is harmful or poisonous to the environment

port a town or city with a harbour for ships to load and unload

source where something begins

spring a place where water flows up out of the ground

stream a small, narrow river that often feeds into a larger river

tide the rise and fall of water in the sea every day

trade buying and selling things

tributary a smaller river or stream that flows into a bigger river

turbine a machine with blades that turn round

valley an area of low ground between hills or mountains

Find out more

Books

Rivers (Kingfisher Readers), Claire Llewellyn (Kingfisher, 2013)

Rivers and Lakes (Amazing Habitats), Leon Gray (Franklin Watts, 2015)

Thames (River Adventures), Paul Manning (Franklin Watts, 2014)

Websites

www.bbc.co.uk/education/topics/zw9k7ty/resources/1
This website has short films giving you a flavour of the UK's rivers.

www.wildlifewatch.org.uk
This website will help you to get involved with helping wildlife, including river wildlife.

Places to visit

Ironbridge Gorge Museums, Ironbridge, Shropshire
www.ironbridge.org.uk
See the historic bridge, discover how to make power from water and step back in time at Blists Hill Victorian Town.

Merseyside Maritime Museum, Liverpool
www.liverpoolmuseums.org.uk/maritime/
Learn about the history of transport on the Mersey.

Thames Barrier Information Centre, Greenwich, London
www.visitlondon.com/things-to-do/place/26941-thames-barrier-information-centre#DxbJtZr8ByCZQ57e.97
Find out more about the Thames Barrier.

Index

BLUE MOON

SOUP

A FAMILY COOKBOOK

Blue Moon Soup

Recipes by **Gary Goss**

Illustrated by **Jane Dyer**

Little, Brown and Company
BOSTON NEW YORK LONDON

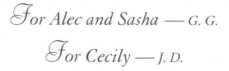

For Alec and Sasha — G. G.

For Cecily — J. D.

Text copyright © 1999 by Gary Goss
Illustrations copyright © 1999 by Jane Dyer

First Edition

Library of Congress Cataloging-in-Publication Data

Goss, Gary.
    Blue moon soup : a family cookbook / recipes by Gary Goss ; illustrated by Jane Dyer.
       p.   cm.
     ISBN 0-316-32991-6
     1. Soups. I. Title.
   TX757.G59 1999
   641.8'13—dc21   98-19458

10 9 8 7 6 5 4 3 2 1

SC

Printed in Hong Kong

The illustrations for this book were done in watercolor on Waterford 140-pound hot press watercolor paper. The text was set in Granjon, and the display type is Liberty.

TURTLE SOUP

Beautiful Soup, so rich and green,
Waiting in a hot tureen!
Who for such dainties would not stoop?
Soup of the evening, beautiful Soup!
Soup of the evening, beautiful Soup!
    Beau—ootiful Soo—oop!
    Beau—ootiful Soo—oop!
Soo—oop of the e—e—evening,
    Beautiful, beautiful Soup!

Beautiful Soup! Who cares for fish,
Game, or any other dish?
Who would not give all else for two p
ennyworth only of beautiful Soup?
Pennyworth only of beautiful Soup?
    Beau—ootiful Soo—oop!
    Beau—ootiful Soo—oop!
Soo—oop of the e—e—evening,
    Beautiful, beauti—FUL SOUP!

— Lewis Carroll

CONTENTS

A Letter from the Chef

Soups are delicious, simple, and fun to make. The recipes in this book are kid-friendly. Children will love the tastes and be proud of the results. The book is designed so that families can quickly cook up a souper meal that will look and taste exquisite.

Soup is versatile—a meal or a prelude to one, hot or cold, hearty or light, and from every culture imaginable. Once you are familiar with these basic recipes, you will be able to use any vegetable in the refrigerator and nearly any spice on hand. So before you go shopping, check to see what's already in the kitchen.

Soup is particularly soothing in the colder months. The aroma of soup simmering on the stove is intoxicating. A bowl of hot and hearty soup takes the chill away and makes you feel warm and good all the way through. These soup days will become memory-filled: a warm house, a loving family, cold weather outside, and hot food inside. Spring soups make use of all that is fresh, new, and sparkling with life. Cold summer soups are refreshing.

The soups in *Blue Moon Soup* are listed seasonally, as suggestions; any soup is good at any time. My wife and I owned the Soup Kitchen Restaurant, in Northampton, Massachusetts, for ten years, and kids loved our soups. Ice Cream Soup is a universal crowd pleaser. Vegetables, such as broccoli in our Brrroccoli Soup au Gratin, take on new, exciting tastes. Use fresh spices and vegetables when available; however, frozen or canned ingredients are fine, to make things easier.

Soups are built around a main vegetable or meat, and usually one dominant spice. For example, Peace Soup's central ingredients are peas and mint. The main spices can be varied according to what you like. If you don't like mint in the Peace Soup, try curry. Taste as you go. If there's not enough flavor, add more seasonings, a little at a time.

To make the most flavorful soups, first sauté the vegetables and spices in melted butter or olive oil, whichever taste you prefer. The broth is added later. This is a quick, easy method. The soup will have an outstanding flavor and delicious aroma, far better than if you had just added the vegetables and spices to the broth.

Always present the soup in a pretty and appetizing way. Decorate the tops of all the soups, salads, and spreads with an attractive garnish.

Ask your mom, dad, or grandparents for a soup recipe. Every family has one that could top these. Every culture has distinctive flavors that make its foods unique. Think about the foods you love best, and see if a soup can be created from them. The possibilities are endless.

What You Will Need

A pot for soup—two to three quarts, with a lid. The pot should be heavy so the soup won't burn.
Additional saucepans
A large skillet

Apron (optional)
Blender
Bread pan
Colander
Cutting board
Flour sifter
Garlic press (optional)
Grater
Ladle
Large mixing bowl
Masher
Measuring spoons and cups

Melon baller (optional)
Microwave oven (optional)
Muffin tin and paper liners
Oven mitts or pot holders
Rubber spatula
Salad bowl
Scrub brush
Spoons, fork, knife
Teapot
Vegetable peeler
Whisk
Wooden spoon

RULES OF THE SOUP KITCHEN

1. Always wash your hands before you begin cooking.
2. Wash all vegetables, too. (They're fun to scrub with a brush!)
3. Assemble all the ingredients before beginning to cook.
4. Have an adult help when using knives, the blender, the oven, or the stove.
5. Use oven mitts when handling anything hot.
6. Turn pot and pan handles to the side when they're on the stove.
7. Never leave the cooking area when the burners are on.
8. Never put foil or metal in a microwave oven.
9. Clean up as you work.
10. If there is an adult standing by to watch the stove, set the table while the soup is cooking.

SETTING THE TABLE

1. Place plates or bowls on the table.
2. The spoon and knife go on the right, with the knife blade facing in.
3. The napkin goes on the left, with the fork on top of it.
4. The glass goes on the right, above the spoon and knife.
5. Place salt, pepper, and soy sauce on the table, too.
6. Flowers and candles are optional, but nice.

WINTER SOUPS

CH-CH-CHILI

Absolutely the best chili. Spicy and flavorful, but without too much "fire."

STUFF:

½ cup dried kidney beans, rinsed, then soaked overnight in 2 cups of water; or 1 cup canned kidney beans

2 tablespoons olive oil

1 pound ground beef

¼ teaspoon crushed red pepper

2 cloves garlic, pressed, or 1 tablespoon garlic powder

2 teaspoons cumin powder

2 teaspoons chili powder

½ teaspoon oregano

½ teaspoon basil

¼ teaspoon salt

1 large onion, chopped

2 large green peppers, chopped

2 cups canned crushed tomatoes

Garnish: grated Parmesan cheese

VEGETARIANS: LEAVE OUT THE MEAT

A note about all dried beans: Rinse them in a colander, and pick out any rocks.

STUFF TO DO:

1. If using dried kidney beans, boil them in 2 cups of water until tender, about 20 minutes. Set aside.
2. In a skillet, heat 1 tablespoon of the olive oil on medium heat.
3. Crumble the ground beef into the skillet, stirring with a wooden spoon.
4. Add half the red pepper, garlic, cumin, chili powder, oregano, basil, and salt and stir.
5. Cook until the ground beef begins to brown, about 5 minutes, then reduce heat.
6. In a soup pot, heat the other tablespoon of olive oil on medium heat.
7. Add the onion, green peppers, and the other half of the spices. Sauté for 5 minutes, stirring occasionally.
8. Add the tomatoes, and simmer another 5 minutes.
9. Add the ground beef mixture, and stir. Reduce heat and simmer for 20 minutes.
10. Just before serving, add the kidney beans. Ladle into bowls and garnish.

Makes four to six servings

Brrroccoli Soup au Gratin

This soup will change your mind about broccoli.

Stuff:

2	tablespoons butter
1	small leek, chopped (1 to 1½ cups)
1	head broccoli, chopped (leave flowers whole)
1	clove garlic, pressed, or 1½ teaspoons garlic powder
¼	teaspoon thyme
⅛	teaspoon nutmeg
¼	teaspoon salt
½	teaspoon pepper
1	stalk celery, chopped
6	ounces sharp cheddar cheese, grated (1½ cups)
2½	cups milk

Garnish: broccoli stalk sunning itself on cheese croutons (page 57)

> To clean leeks, cut off the dark green part at the very top. Make one lengthwise cut to open. Separate and wash thoroughly.

Stuff to Do:

1. Melt the butter in a soup pot on medium heat.
2. Add the leek, half of the broccoli, the garlic, thyme, nutmeg, salt, and pepper. Sauté for 5 minutes, stirring with a wooden spoon.
3. Add the rest of the broccoli, the celery, and just enough water to cover the vegetables (about 2 cups), and stir.
4. Bring to a boil, then reduce heat and simmer, covered, until the vegetables are tender, about 15 to 20 minutes.
5. Add the cheese, and stir until well blended.
6. In a blender or a large bowl, blend or mash 2 cups of the soup with the milk until thick and silky smooth.
7. Return the blended soup to the soup pot, and stir to mix. (Once milk or cream is added to a soup, don't let it boil.)
8. Ladle into bowls and garnish.

Makes four to six servings

If blender gets too full, blend in batches.

FISH SOUP

For an even sweeter chowder, try mussels and a touch of saffron.

STUFF:

2   medium potatoes, peeled and chopped

2   dozen steamer or quahog clams, scrubbed clean with a brush

3   tablespoons butter

1   small to medium onion, chopped

2   tablespoons cooking sherry or dry white wine (optional)

½   teaspoon thyme

½   teaspoon dry mustard

¼   teaspoon salt

½   teaspoon pepper

½   stalk celery, chopped

3   cups heavy cream

     Garnish: Goldfish crackers and parsley sprigs

> Note: You will need 3 saucepans for this recipe.

STUFF TO DO:

1. Boil the potatoes in 3 cups of water until tender, about 15 minutes. Drain them, set them aside, and save the broth for another soup.

2. In a colander, rinse the clams with cold water. Place them in a saucepan with just enough water to cover them (about 2 cups) and 1 tablespoon of the butter. Bring to a boil, and continue to boil until the clams open, about 5 minutes. Remove the clams from their shells, save the broth, and set both aside.

3. Melt the remaining 2 tablespoons of butter in a soup pot on medium heat.

4. Add the onion, sherry if using, thyme, mustard, salt, and pepper. Sauté for 5 minutes, stirring with a wooden spoon.

5. Add the celery and clam broth, and stir.

6. Bring to a boil, then reduce heat and simmer for about 15 minutes.

7. Add the potatoes, clams, and cream, and keep stirring. This is supposed to be a thin cream soup, but if it looks too thin, mash ½ cup of the potatoes with a masher or blend some of the soup in a blender until thick and silky smooth, then return it to the pot and stir it in.

8. Ladle into bowls and garnish.

Makes four to six servings

HOT DIGGITY DOG SOUP

The traditional way to make this minestrone soup is with prosciutto or a ham bone. It can also be vegetarian—just leave out the dog.

STUFF:

⅓   cup dried kidney beans, rinsed, then soaked overnight in 2 cups of water; or ½ cup canned kidney beans

½   cup elbow macaroni

2   hot dogs, microwaved for about 2 minutes or boiled for 5 minutes

2   teaspoons olive oil

1   small onion, chopped

½   green pepper, sliced

2   cloves garlic, pressed, or 1 tablespoon garlic powder

½   teaspoon oregano

½   teaspoon basil

¼   teaspoon salt

½   teaspoon pepper

Note: You will need 3 saucepans for this recipe.

1   cup canned crushed tomatoes

½   stalk celery, chopped

1   carrot, chopped

⅓   cup frozen chopped spinach

Garnish: grated Parmesan cheese and parsley sprigs

STUFF TO DO:

1. If using dried kidney beans, boil them in 2 cups of water until tender, about 20 minutes. Drain, save the broth, and set the beans aside.
2. Boil the macaroni in 5 cups of water until tender, about 20 minutes (check instructions). Drain and set aside.
3. Slice the cooked hot dogs into rounds and set them aside.
4. Heat the olive oil in a soup pot on medium heat.
5. Add the onion, green pepper, garlic, oregano, basil, salt, and pepper. Sauté for 5 minutes, stirring with a wooden spoon.
6. Add the tomatoes and stir.

> Cut the carrot lengthwise, then slice into half-moons so it will cook as quickly as the other vegetables.

7. Add the celery, carrot, and spinach, and stir.
8. Add the kidney bean broth and 4 cups of water.
9. Bring to a boil, then reduce heat and simmer, covered, for 20 minutes.
10. For more flavor and lighter color, blend ½ cup of the soup in a blender until thick and silky smooth, then return it to the soup pot and stir.
11. Just before serving, add the kidney beans, hot dog slices, and macaroni.
12. Ladle into bowls and garnish.

   Makes four to six servings

TWIST & SHOUT

John Lennon's great remake of the original. Try adding noodles or rice to other soups in this book, too.

STUFF:

⅓   cup twist noodles

2   tablespoons butter

1   small onion, chopped

1   cup chopped mushrooms

1   teaspoon fresh lemon juice

1   clove garlic, pressed, or 1½ teaspoons garlic powder

½   teaspoon basil

½   teaspoon salt

½   teaspoon pepper

1   cup canned crushed tomatoes

1   carrot, chopped

     Garnish: fresh basil and popped popcorn

STUFF TO DO:

1. Boil the noodles in 3 cups of water until tender, about 15 minutes (check instructions). Drain and set aside.
2. Cook some popcorn, following the directions on the package. Snack on some while you cook, and save the rest for garnish.
3. Melt the butter in a soup pot on medium heat.
4. Add the onion, mushrooms, lemon juice, garlic, basil, salt, and pepper. Sauté for 5 minutes, stirring with a wooden spoon.
5. Add the tomatoes, carrot, and 6 cups of water, and stir.
6. Bring to a boil, then reduce heat and simmer, covered, for 20 minutes.
7. In a blender or a bowl, blend or mash ½ cup of the soup until thick and silky smooth, then return it to the soup pot and stir.
8. Add the noodles and stir.
9. Ladle into bowls and garnish.
     Makes four to six servings

Sob Soup

"Onion soup sustains. The process of making it is somewhat like the process of learning to love. It requires commitment, extraordinary effort, time, and will make you cry." —Ronni Lundy, Esquire

Stuff:

1   cup croutons (page 57)
2   tablespoons butter
1   tablespoon cooking sherry or dry white wine (optional)
2   teaspoons fresh lemon juice
2   cloves garlic, pressed, or 1 tablespoon garlic powder
½   teaspoon pepper
2   large onions, sliced and halved
2   beef or vegetable bouillon cubes
6   ounces Gruyère cheese, grated (1 cup)

Stuff to Do:

1. Make the croutons.
2. Preheat the oven to 400°F.
3. Melt the butter in a soup pot on medium heat.
4. Add the sherry if using, lemon juice, garlic, pepper, and half of the onions. Sauté for 5 minutes, stirring with a wooden spoon.
5. Add the remaining onions, and stir.
6. Add 6 cups of water and the bouillon cubes.
7. Bring to a boil, then reduce heat and simmer, covered, for 15 minutes.
8. Ladle into individual crocks.
9. Sprinkle some croutons and cheese on top of each crockful.
10. Bake for 15 to 20 minutes, until lightly golden and bubbly.

Makes four to six servings

PEACE SOUP

Always search and work for peace and friendship. A great start is through cooking this pea soup.

STUFF:

2   tablespoons butter

1   small leek, chopped (1 to 1½ cups)

1   teaspoon minced fresh mint or 1 teaspoon curry powder (2 teaspoons if you love curry)

½   teaspoon grated fresh ginger or ⅛ teaspoon powdered (optional)

¼   teaspoon salt

½   teaspoon pepper

1   10-ounce package frozen peas

1   carrot, chopped

½   stalk celery, chopped

2½   cups milk

Garnish: fresh mint or carrot curls

> *Use leeks in cream soups instead of onions. Leeks taste sweeter.*

STUFF TO DO:

1. Melt the butter in a soup pot on medium heat.
2. Add the leek, mint, ginger if using, salt, and pepper. Sauté for about 5 minutes, stirring with a wooden spoon.
3. Add the peas, carrot, celery, and just enough water to cover them (about 2 cups), and stir.
4. Bring to a boil, then reduce heat and simmer, covered, until the vegetables are tender, about 15 to 20 minutes.
5. In a blender or a large bowl, blend or mash 2 cups of the soup with the milk until thick and silky smooth.
6. Return the blended soup to the soup pot, and stir.
7. Ladle into bowls and garnish.

Makes four to six servings

ZERO-ZERO SOUP

An ancient (1960s) Chinese version of hot and sour soup. It's the cornstarch that gives this soup its strange jelled, oozy look.

STUFF:

KEEP FRESH GINGER IN THE FREEZER

2	teaspoons hot sesame oil
1½	tablespoons soy sauce
⅓	cup chopped scallions
1	cup sliced shiitake mushrooms
1	teaspoon white wine vinegar
2	cloves garlic, pressed, or 1 tablespoon garlic powder
1	teaspoon grated fresh ginger or ¼ teaspoon powdered
½	teaspoon pepper
⅓	cup water chestnuts
⅓	cup snow peas
⅓	cup chopped bok choy
⅓	cup chopped bamboo shoots
5	cups chicken broth, or 2 chicken bouillon cubes in 5 cups boiling water
2	tablespoons cornstarch dissolved in ½ cup cold water
⅓	cup firm tofu (⅓ of a cake), chopped into bite-size pieces

Garnish: ¼ cup chopped scallions

STUFF TO DO:

1. Heat the sesame oil and soy sauce in a soup pot on medium heat.
2. Add the scallions, mushrooms, vinegar, garlic, ginger, and pepper. Cook for 2 minutes, stirring with a wooden spoon.
3. Add the water chestnuts, snow peas, bok choy, and bamboo shoots, and stir.
4. Add the chicken broth, and bring to a boil.
5. Stir in the cornstarch. Add the tofu. Simmer, covered, until vegetables are tender, about 20 minutes.
6. Ladle into bowls and garnish.

Makes four to six servings

POLKA DOT SOUP

Makes a fashion statement—this Cuban black bean soup looks just as good on your shirt as in your bowl.

STUFF:

1   cup dried black beans, rinsed, then soaked overnight in 3 cups of water; or 2 cups canned black beans

1   tablespoon butter

2   cloves garlic, pressed, or 1 tablespoon garlic powder

½   leek, chopped

1   red bell pepper, chopped

½   teaspoon cumin powder

¼   teaspoon thyme

¼   teaspoon salt

½   teaspoon pepper

1   teaspoon fresh lemon juice

1   tablespoon cooking sherry (optional)

½   stalk celery, chopped

Garnish: a dollop of sour cream or yogurt and a slice of lemon

> *Beans will double in size when cooked. Bean soups constantly eat up broth, so add water, a half cup at a time, as needed. Beans are cooked when tender.*

STUFF TO DO:

1. If using dried beans, boil them in 6 cups of water in a soup pot until the beans are tender and beginning to turn mushy, about 25 minutes. If using canned beans, just add in step 6.
2. In a separate pot, melt the butter over medium heat.
3. Add the garlic, leek, red pepper, cumin, thyme, salt, pepper, lemon juice, and sherry if using. Sauté for 5 minutes, stirring with a wooden spoon.
4. Add the celery and 2 cups of water, and stir.
5. Bring to a boil, then reduce heat and simmer, covered, for 15 minutes.
6. Add the vegetable mixture to the beans, and stir.
7. In a blender or a bowl, blend or mash ½ cup of the soup until thick and silky smooth, then return it to the soup pot and stir.
8. Ladle into bowls and garnish.

Makes four to six servings

SPRING SOUPS

Spring Chicken Soup

"You ain't no spring chicken, but you sure know how to strut your stuff." —*Taj Mahal*

STUFF:

1	medium-size chicken (about 6 pounds), whole, with skin on
1	large onion
3	carrots
2	stalks celery
1	tablespoon chopped parsley
2	cloves garlic
1	bay leaf
¼	teaspoon tarragon
½	teaspoon salt
½	teaspoon pepper
1	cup egg noodles

Garnish: parsley sprigs

> Also known as "Jewish penicillin"— tastes great when you feel bad, because it's cooked with love. Chicken soup is a great form of nourishment.

STUFF TO DO:

1. Combine all the ingredients except the noodles in 10 cups of cold water.
2. Bring to a gentle boil, and skim off the foam that comes to the top.
3. Continue to skim the foam until it no longer appears.
4. Reduce heat and simmer, uncovered, for 2 hours.
5. Boil the noodles in 5 cups of water until tender, about 15 minutes, then drain and set aside.
6. When the soup is cooked, remove the chicken and vegetables with a strainer. Cut the chicken meat into bite-size pieces, discarding the skin and bones. Cut the carrots and celery in half, and put some meat, carrot, and celery in each bowl. (Leave out the onion.) Add some noodles to each bowl, ladle in the soup, and garnish.

Makes four to six servings

> To create a basic chicken broth, follow steps 1 through 4, then strain out the chicken and vegetables.

BOUNCY, BOUNCY BALL SOUP

You won't want these matzo balls to bounce too high. The great matzo ball debate: heavy or light?

STUFF:

 5 cups chicken broth (page 16)

Matzo Balls
 2 tablespoons vegetable oil
 2 large eggs, lightly beaten
 ½ cup matzo meal
 ¼ teaspoon salt
 ¼ teaspoon pepper
 3 tablespoons chicken broth
 Garnish: parsley sprigs

STUFF TO DO:

1. In a large bowl, whisk the oil and eggs.
2. Combine the matzo meal, salt, and pepper with the egg mixture.
3. Add the 3 tablespoons of chicken broth, and mix.
4. Cover and refrigerate for 15 minutes.
5. Boil 1½ quarts of water in a pot.
6. Form the matzo dough into balls about 1 inch in diameter, and drop them into the lightly boiling water.
7. Simmer, covered, for 30 minutes.
8. Serve with chicken broth, and garnish.
 Makes four to six servings

(No) Duck Soup

Groucho Marx's favorite lentil soup.

Stuff:

1	cup dried lentils, cleaned and rinsed
2	tablespoons butter
1	small onion, chopped
2	teaspoons fresh lemon juice
1	clove garlic, pressed, or 1½ teaspoons garlic powder
1	teaspoon tarragon
¼	teaspoon salt
½	teaspoon pepper
1	small carrot, chopped
½	stalk celery, chopped
½	cup canned crushed tomatoes

Garnish: parsley sprigs

Stuff to Do:

1. Boil the lentils in 6 cups of water until the lentils are tender, about 20 minutes. Set aside.
2. Melt the butter in a soup pot on medium heat.
3. Add the onion, lemon juice, garlic, tarragon, salt, and pepper. Sauté for 5 minutes, stirring with a wooden spoon.
4. Add the carrot and celery, and stir.
5. Add the tomatoes and 1 cup of water. Bring to a boil, then reduce heat and simmer, covered, until vegetables are tender, about 15 minutes.
6. Transfer the tomato mixture to the lentil pot, and stir. Simmer for an additional 10 minutes.
7. Ladle into bowls and garnish.

Makes four to six servings

ABRACADABRA

Add lemon, egg, and rice to leftover chicken broth . . . and abra-cadabra—Greek Lemon-and-Egg Soup!

STUFF:

5   cups chicken broth (page 16) or 2 chicken bouillon cubes
      in 5 cups of boiling water

⅔   cup rice

1   egg

½   lemon at room temperature
      Garnish: lemon slice

> *Warm lemons will give you twice as much juice as cold ones.*

STUFF TO DO:

1. Heat the chicken broth in a soup pot on medium heat.
2. Cook the rice according to the directions on the box, and set it aside.
3. Whip the egg.
4. When the chicken broth is very hot but not boiling, slowly stir in the egg.
5. Squeeze in juice from the lemon.
6. Add the rice.
7. Ladle into bowls and garnish.

    Makes four to six servings

SOUP OF THE EVENING

Feta cheese becomes sweet when cooked in this very rich spinach soup.

STUFF:

2	tablespoons butter
1	small leek, chopped (1 to 1½ cups)
½	teaspoon pepper
1	garlic clove, pressed, or 1½ teaspoons garlic powder
1	pinch nutmeg . . . ouch!
½	stalk celery, chopped
1	10-ounce package frozen chopped spinach
1½	cups crumbled salty feta cheese
2½	cups milk

Garnish: cheese croutons (page 57) and/or fresh spinach leaf

STUFF TO DO:

1. Melt the butter in a soup pot on medium heat.
2. Add the leek, pepper, garlic, and nutmeg, and sauté for 5 minutes, stirring with a wooden spoon.
3. Add the celery, spinach, and just enough water to cover the vegetables (about 2 cups), and stir.
4. Bring to a boil, then reduce heat and simmer, covered, until the celery is tender, about 15 minutes.
5. Add the feta cheese, and stir until blended.
6. In a blender or a bowl, blend or mash 2 cups of the soup with the milk until thick and silky smooth.
7. Return the blended soup to the soup pot, and stir.
8. Ladle into bowls and garnish.

Makes four to six servings

MARY HAD A LITTLE LAMB STEW

BAA! Vegetarians may leave out the lamb.

STUFF:

- 2 tablespoons butter
- 1 pound lamb shoulder or leg, cut into cubes
- 1 medium onion, chopped
- 2 cloves garlic, pressed, or 1 tablespoon garlic powder
- 1 tablespoon chopped parsley
- ½ teaspoon sage
- ½ teaspoon thyme
- ½ teaspoon salt
- ½ teaspoon pepper
- 1 stalk celery, chopped
- 1 potato, peeled and chopped
- 1 cup chopped mushrooms
- 1 carrot, chopped
- ½ cup canned crushed tomatoes or 10 cherry tomatoes
- ½ cup frozen peas
  Garnish: parsley sprigs

STUFF TO DO:

1. Melt the butter in a soup pot on medium heat.
2. Add the lamb, onion, garlic, parsley, sage, thyme, salt, and pepper. Sauté for 10 minutes, stirring with a wooden spoon.
3. Add the celery, potato, mushrooms, carrot, and 2 cups of water, and stir.
4. Bring to a boil, then reduce heat and simmer, covered, for 1½ hours.
5. Ten minutes before serving, add the tomatoes and peas.
6. Ladle into bowls and garnish.
   Makes four to six servings

FULL MOON SOUP

An old Yorkshire maid's tale says that after eating a hot kale potion, you'll see the man you will marry. Try this Portuguese kale soup!

STUFF:

- ⅓ cup dried kidney beans, rinsed, then soaked overnight in 3 cups of water; or ½ cup canned kidney beans
- 1 tablespoon olive oil
- 1 small onion, chopped
- ½ green pepper, chopped
- ½ stalk celery, chopped
- 1 carrot, chopped
- 1 cup chopped kale
- ½ teaspoon basil
- ½ teaspoon oregano
- ¼ teaspoon salt
- ½ teaspoon pepper
- 1 cup canned crushed tomatoes
- 2 pieces *linguica* (Portuguese sausage), sliced into rounds
  Garnish: kale and grated Parmesan cheese

STUFF TO DO:

1. If using dried kidney beans, boil them in 2 cups of water until tender, about 20 minutes. Drain, save the broth, and set the beans aside.
2. Heat the olive oil in a soup pot on medium heat.
3. Add the onion, green pepper, celery, carrot, ½ cup of the kale, the basil, oregano, salt, and pepper. Sauté for 5 minutes, stirring with a wooden spoon.
4. Add the tomatoes and *linguica*. Sauté for about 5 minutes.
5. Add the remaining kale, the kidney bean broth, and 4 cups of water, and stir.
6. Bring to a boil, then reduce heat and simmer, covered, for 20 minutes.
7. In a blender or a bowl, blend or mash ½ cup of the soup until thick and silky smooth, then return it to the soup pot and stir. Add the kidney beans and stir.
8. Ladle into bowls and garnish.
   Makes four to six servings

SWEET DREAMS SOUP

Hot carrot soup in your belly at night feels good and soothing. . . .
Sweet dreams!

STUFF:

1   small potato, peeled and chopped
2   tablespoons butter
1   small leek, chopped (1 to 1½ cups)
2   large carrots, finely chopped
½   teaspoon grated fresh ginger or ⅛ teaspoon powdered; or ½ teaspoon
    curry
¼   teaspoon thyme
⅛   teaspoon nutmeg
¼   teaspoon salt
½   teaspoon pepper
½   stalk celery, chopped
2½   cups milk

Garnish: carrot curls and croutons (page 57)

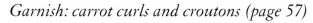

STUFF TO DO:

1. Boil the potato in 2 cups of water until tender, about 15 minutes. Drain, save the broth, and set the potato aside.
2. Melt the butter in a soup pot on medium heat.
3. Add the leek, half the carrots, the ginger, thyme, nutmeg, salt, and pepper. Sauté for 5 minutes, stirring with a wooden spoon.
4. Add the celery, the remaining carrots, the cooked potato, and the potato broth.
5. Add 1 cup water, and stir.
6. Bring to a boil, then reduce heat and simmer, covered, until the carrots are tender, about 20 minutes.
7. In a blender or a bowl, blend or mash 2 cups of the soup with the milk until thick and silky smooth.
8. Return the blended soup to the soup pot, and stir.
9. Ladle into bowls and garnish.

Makes four to six servings

25

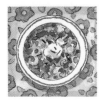

SUMMER SOLSTICE SOUP

Summer solstice—the longest day of the year—is the first official day of summer, a good day for vegetable soup.

STUFF:

1   potato, peeled and chopped
2   tablespoons butter
1   small onion, chopped
1   tablespoon chopped parsley
1   clove garlic, pressed, or 1½ teaspoons garlic powder
½   teaspoon rosemary
½   teaspoon salt
½   teaspoon pepper
2   fresh tomatoes, crushed or blended, or 1 cup canned crushed tomatoes
½   stalk celery, chopped
1   carrot, chopped
1   of anything from the garden (your choice), chopped
    Garnish: fresh rosemary and a dollop of sour cream

STUFF To Do:

1. Boil the potato in 2 cups of water until tender, about 15 minutes. Drain, save the broth, and set the potato aside.
2. Melt the butter in a soup pot on medium heat.
3. Add the onion, parsley, garlic, rosemary, salt, and pepper. Sauté for 5 minutes, stirring with a wooden spoon.
4. Add the tomatoes, celery, carrot, garden item of your choice, potato, and potato broth, and stir.
5. Add 3 cups of water, and bring to a boil, then reduce heat and simmer, covered, for 20 minutes.
6. In a blender or a bowl, blend or mash ½ cup of the soup until thick and silky smooth, then return it to the soup pot and stir.
7. Ladle into bowls and garnish.
   Makes four to six servings

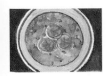

BEST BUDDY SOUP

Two very different tastes—tomatoes and oranges—come together.

STUFF:

2   tablespoons butter
1   small leek, chopped (1 to 1½ cups)
¼   green pepper, chopped
2   cups canned crushed tomatoes or 3 to 4 fresh tomatoes, crushed or
       blended
1   orange at room temperature, cut in half
½   teaspoon basil
⅛   teaspoon tarragon
1   teaspoon chopped parsley
¼   teaspoon salt
½   teaspoon pepper
1½   cups half-and-half or milk
       Garnish: thin orange rounds

STUFF TO DO:

1. Melt the butter in a soup pot on medium heat.
2. Add the leek, green pepper, ½ cup of the tomatoes, juice from one of the orange halves, the basil, tarragon, parsley, salt, and pepper. Sauté for 5 minutes, stirring with a wooden spoon.
3. Add the remaining tomatoes and the juice from the other orange half.
4. Add 1½ cups of water, and stir.
5. Bring to a boil, then reduce heat and simmer for 15 minutes.
6. In a blender or a bowl, blend or mash 2 cups of the soup with the half-and-half until thick and silky smooth.
7. Return the blended soup to the soup pot, and stir.
8. Ladle into bowls and garnish.
   Makes four to six servings

HOW DOES YOUR GARDEN GROW?
SOUP

HOW DOES YOUR GARDEN GROW?

Gazpacho—fresh and zesty from the garden.

STUFF:

1	green pepper, roughly chopped
1	medium onion, chopped
1	cucumber, peeled and roughly chopped
1½	cups canned crushed tomatoes or 3 fresh tomatoes
1	tablespoon red wine vinegar
1	tablespoon olive oil
1	tablespoon fresh lemon juice
1	tablespoon chopped parsley
1	clove garlic, pressed, or 1½ teaspoons garlic powder
¼	teaspoon cayenne pepper
½	teaspoon salt

Garnish: sprouts—you can grow these indoors all year round

STUFF TO DO:

1. In a blender, blend the green pepper and onion with ½ cup water, then pour into a large container.
2. Blend everything else with ½ cup water, then add it to the green-pepper-and-onion mixture. If the soup is too thick, add another ½ cup water.
3. Pour into bowls and garnish.

Makes four to six servings

YOU CAN'T ELOPE

Sweet and smooth cantaloupe soup, with just a dab of yogurt.
As good as an old-fashioned Creamsicle on a hot summer day.

STUFF:

1	small cantaloupe, sliced in half and seeded
½	cup half-and-half
1	teaspoon dry white wine (optional)
1	teaspoon orange or fresh lemon juice
1	dash vanilla (optional)
1	teaspoon grated fresh ginger or ¼ teaspoon powdered
1½	teaspoons chopped fresh mint

Garnish: yogurt, melon balls, and raspberries

STUFF TO DO:

1. Using a melon baller or teaspoon, make one-quarter of the cantaloupe into melon balls. Set aside.
2. Cut the rest of the cantaloupe into large pieces. In a blender or a bowl, blend or mash it with 1½ cups water, the half-and-half, wine if using, orange juice, vanilla if using, ginger, and mint.
3. Pour into bowls and garnish.

Makes four to six servings

BELIEVE IT OR NOT!

Ice cream soup—what a treat! How simple can you get?

STUFF:

4 to 6 big scoops of the ice cream of your choice
¼ cup chocolate syrup or hot fudge
½ pint of whipping cream, whipped
Garnish: raspberries

STUFF TO DO:

1. Scoop the ice cream into bowls, and let it melt.
2. With the chocolate syrup, make a pretty design on top of each serving.
3. Add a dollop of the whipped cream to each serving, and garnish.

Makes four to six servings

JOIE DE VICHYSSOISE

My favorite—either hot or cold. This soup was invented when King Louis XIV, afraid of being poisoned, had his leek and potato soup tested by a number of tasters. He sent it back because it wasn't hot enough. The chef returned it as cold vichyssoise.

STUFF:

3	medium potatoes, peeled and chopped
2	tablespoons butter
1	large leek, chopped
1	medium onion, chopped
1	pinch dill
½	teaspoon salt
½	teaspoon pepper
2½	cups milk

Garnish: parsley sprigs or dill

STUFF TO DO:

1. Boil the potatoes in 3 cups of water until tender, about 15 minutes. Drain, save the broth, and set the potatoes aside.
2. Melt the butter in a soup pot on medium heat.
3. Add the leek, onion, dill, salt, and pepper. Sauté for 5 minutes, stirring with a wooden spoon.
4. Add the potatoes and broth, and stir.
5. Bring to a boil, then reduce heat and simmer for 15 minutes.
6. In a blender, blend the soup with the milk until thick and silky smooth.
7. Refrigerate until cool.
8. Pour or ladle into bowls and garnish.

Makes four to six servings

SERVE WARM IF YOU CAN'T WAIT

RATATATATOUILLE

Can't you just see drummer Gene Krupa doing a solo?

STUFF:

1	tablespoon olive oil
1	small onion, chopped
½	red bell pepper, chopped
1	small eggplant, or ½ of a large one, chopped
2	cloves garlic, pressed, or 1 tablespoon garlic powder
½	teaspoon basil
¼	teaspoon oregano
½	teaspoon salt
½	teaspoon pepper
1	cup canned crushed tomatoes or 3 fresh tomatoes, crushed or blended
1	carrot, chopped
1	yellow squash, sliced
½	cup sliced mushrooms

Garnish: grated Parmesan cheese and croutons (page 57)

STUFF TO DO:

1. Heat the olive oil in a soup pot on medium heat.
2. Add the onion, red pepper, half of the eggplant, the garlic, basil, oregano, salt, and pepper. Sauté for 5 minutes, stirring with a wooden spoon.
3. Add the rest of the eggplant, tomatoes, carrot, squash, mushrooms, and 6 cups of water, and stir.
4. Bring to a boil, then reduce heat and simmer, covered, for 20 minutes.
5. In a blender or a bowl, blend or mash ½ cup of the soup until thick and silky smooth, then return it to the soup pot and stir.
6. Ladle into bowls and garnish.

Makes four to six servings

BISQUE IN THE SUN

A bisque is a cream soup with shellfish.

STUFF:

2	tablespoons butter
1	small leek, chopped (1 to 1½ cups)
3	cups canned crushed tomatoes or 5 fresh tomatoes, crushed or blended
½	teaspoon fresh lemon juice
½	teaspoon cooking sherry or dry white wine (optional)
½	teaspoon chopped cilantro
¼	teaspoon salt
½	teaspoon pepper
½	stalk celery, chopped
1½	cups half-and-half or milk

Garnish: shrimp (two per bowl) bisquing in the sun on croutons (page 57)

STUFF TO DO:

1. To prepare the garnish, peel and clean the shrimp, then boil them in ½ cup water for 3 to 4 minutes. Drain, and set aside.
2. Melt the butter in a soup pot on medium heat.
3. Add the leek, 1 cup of the tomatoes, the lemon juice, sherry if using, cilantro, salt, and pepper. Sauté for 5 minutes, stirring with a wooden spoon.
4. Add the celery, the remaining tomatoes, and 1 cup water, and stir.
5. Bring to a boil, then reduce heat and simmer until celery is tender, about 15 minutes.
6. In a blender or a bowl, blend or mash 2 cups of the soup with the half-and-half until thick and silky smooth.
7. Return the blended soup to the soup pot, and stir.
8. Ladle into bowls and garnish.

Makes four to six servings

LICKITY SPLIT PEA SOUP

Doesn't cook quite as fast as its name, but the taste is well worth the wait.

STUFF:

1	cup split peas, rinsed, then soaked overnight in 3 cups of water
2	tablespoons butter
1	small leek or onion, chopped
¼	teaspoon salt
½	teaspoon pepper
¼	teaspoon thyme
1	teaspoon chopped parsley
½	stalk celery, chopped
1	carrot, chopped
½	cup frozen peas

Garnish: carrot curls or parsley sprigs

STUFF TO DO:

1. Boil the split peas in 6 cups of water. Cook until the peas are mushy, about 25 minutes. Set aside.
2. Melt the butter in a medium saucepan on medium heat.
3. Add the leek, salt, pepper, thyme, and parsley, and sauté for 5 minutes, stirring with a wooden spoon.
4. Add the celery, carrot, and 2 cups of water, and stir.
5. Bring to a boil, then reduce the heat and simmer, covered, for 15 minutes.
6. Add the vegetable mixture and the peas to the split pea pot, and simmer for 5 minutes.
7. Ladle into bowls and garnish.

Makes four to six servings

ONE POTATO, TWO POTATO

A fair way to choose sides — also known as Philadelphia Pepper Pot.

STUFF:

3	medium potatoes, peeled and chopped
2	tablespoons butter
1	small leek, chopped (1 to 1½ cups)
1	green pepper, chopped
1	tablespoon chopped parsley
½	teaspoon salt
½	teaspoon pepper

Potatoes should be boiled separately; the broth tastes great and is used to thicken soups.

Garnish: bacon bits (from 6 slices cooked bacon) with bread crumbs or croutons (page 57)

STUFF TO DO:

1. Boil the potatoes in 5 cups of water until tender, about 15 minutes. Drain, save the broth, and set the potatoes aside.
2. Heat the butter in a soup pot on medium heat. (Alternatively, if you are making your bacon bits for the garnish right before making the soup, cook the bacon in the soup pot, then discard most of the grease, leaving enough to sauté the soup ingredients in.)
3. Add the leek, green pepper, parsley, salt, and pepper. Sauté for 5 minutes, stirring with a wooden spoon.
4. Add half of the potatoes and half of the broth, and stir.
5. Bring to a boil, then reduce heat and simmer for 15 minutes.
6. In a blender or a bowl, blend or mash 1 cup of the soup until thick and silky smooth. If the soup is too thick to blend, add another ½ cup of potato broth.
7. Return the blended soup to the soup pot. Add the rest of the cooled potatoes and broth, and stir.
8. Ladle into bowls and garnish.
   Makes four to six servings

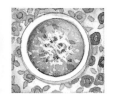

PETER, PETER, PUMPKIN EATER

Although both of its main ingredients come from cans, this corn and pumpkin chowder is still delicious and unique.

STUFF:

1	medium potato, peeled and chopped
2	tablespoons butter
1	small leek, chopped (1 to 1½ cups)
1	tablespoon cooking sherry or dry white wine (optional)
½	teaspoon dry mustard
¼	teaspoon saffron (optional)
¼	teaspoon salt
½	teaspoon pepper
1	cup canned pumpkin
½	carrot, chopped
1¼	cups canned creamed corn
2½	cups milk

Garnish: shredded Muenster cheese (1½ cups) and parsley sprigs

STUFF TO DO:

1. Boil the potato in 2 cups of water until tender, about 15 minutes. Drain, save the broth, and set the potato aside.
2. Melt the butter in a soup pot on medium heat.
3. Add the leek, cooking sherry if using, mustard, saffron if using, salt, and pepper. Sauté for 5 minutes, stirring with a wooden spoon.
4. Add the potato, its broth, the pumpkin, carrot, half of the corn, and 2 cups of water, and stir.
5. Bring to a boil, then reduce heat and simmer, covered, for 15 minutes.
6. In a blender or a bowl, blend or mash half the soup with the milk until thick and silky smooth.
7. Return the blended soup to the soup pot, and stir.
8. Add the remaining corn and stir. Ladle into bowls and garnish.
   OR: Ladle into crocks or baked pumpkin or squash shells, garnish, place on a cookie sheet, and bake at 400°F until bubbling and lightly browned on top.
   Makes four to six servings

WILD THYME SOUP

The combination of thyme, lemon, and soy with mushrooms and barley . . . outstanding!

STUFF:

⅓ cup barley
6 tablespoons soy sauce
2 tablespoons butter
1 small onion, chopped
½ green pepper, chopped
3 to 4 cups chopped mushrooms
1 tablespoon fresh lemon juice
2 cloves garlic, pressed, or 1 tablespoon garlic powder
½ teaspoon thyme
½ teaspoon pepper
½ stalk celery, chopped
1 carrot, chopped
Garnish: sliced mushrooms

Barley eats up water, so check the water level and stir. If needed, add another cup of water.

STUFF TO DO:

1. Boil the barley in 4 cups of water and 3 tablespoons of the soy sauce for about 20 minutes. Drain, save the broth, and set the barley aside.
2. Melt the butter in a soup pot on medium heat.
3. Add the onion, green pepper, mushrooms, lemon juice, garlic, thyme, and pepper. Sauté for 5 minutes, stirring with a wooden spoon.
4. Add the celery, carrot, the remaining 3 tablespoons of soy sauce, and 4 cups of water, and stir.
5. Bring to a boil, then reduce heat and simmer, covered, for 15 minutes.
6. Add the barley and its broth, and stir.
7. Simmer for an additional 15 minutes.
8. Ladle into bowls and garnish.
Makes four to six servings

SQUISH-SQUASH SOUP

You gotta squish the squash, or it ain't no soup, no jive!

STUFF:

2 tablespoons butter
1 small leek, chopped (1 to 1½ cups)
1 butternut squash, peeled and cubed
1 teaspoon dry white wine or ½ teaspoon cooking sherry (optional)
1 pinch nutmeg
¼ teaspoon salt
½ teaspoon pepper
1 carrot, chopped
¼ cup chopped fresh chives
2½ cups milk
Garnish: chopped fresh chives

STUFF TO DO:

1. Melt the butter in a soup pot on medium heat.
2. Add the leek, half of the squash, the wine if using, nutmeg, salt, and pepper. Sauté for 5 minutes, stirring with a wooden spoon.
3. Add the carrot, chives, remaining squash, and 2 cups of water, and stir.
4. Bring to a boil, then reduce heat and simmer, covered, for 20 minutes.
5. In a blender or a bowl, blend or mash half the soup with the milk until thick and silky smooth.
6. Return the blended soup to the soup pot, and stir.
7. Ladle into bowls and garnish.

Makes four to six servings

45

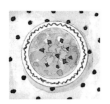

HEY, HEY SOUP

This hot and jazzy sweet potato soup is named after a great jazz club in Kansas City.

STUFF:

- 2 tablespoons butter
- 1 small leek, chopped (1 to 1½ cups)
- ¼ cup chopped chives
- ¾ cup sliced mushrooms
- 2 large sweet potatoes, peeled and thinly sliced (ask an adult to slice)
- 1 tablespoon cooking sherry or dry white wine (optional)
- 1 teaspoon curry
- ¼ teaspoon salt
- ½ teaspoon pepper
- 2 cups milk

  Garnish: 1 cup shredded Muenster cheese, ¼ cup sliced mushrooms, and 1 bar of great chocolate, broken into bite-size pieces

STUFF TO DO:

1. Preheat the oven to 400°F.
2. Melt the butter in a soup pot on medium heat.
3. Add the leek, chives, mushrooms, half of the sweet potatoes, the sherry if using, curry, salt, and pepper. Sauté for 10 minutes, stirring with a wooden spoon.
4. Add the remaining sweet potatoes and 2 cups of water, and stir.
5. Bring to a boil, then reduce heat and simmer, covered, for 15 minutes.
6. In a blender or a bowl, blend or mash half the soup with the milk until thick and silky smooth.
7. Return the blended soup to the soup pot, and stir.
8. Place soup crocks on a cookie sheet. Ladle soup into crocks, and garnish. Bake for 10 to 15 minutes, until lightly browned and bubbly.

   Makes four to six servings

FUNNY FACE SOUP

Named after a great Audrey Hepburn movie. I got this cabbage soup recipe from my mother. Ask your family members for some of their favorite recipes.

STUFF:

2	tablespoons butter
2	small onions, chopped
½	green pepper, chopped
3	tablespoons fresh lemon juice
1	clove garlic, pressed, or 1½ teaspoons garlic powder
½	teaspoon salt
½	teaspoon pepper
1	small head of cabbage, chopped
1½	cups canned crushed tomatoes

Garnish: sour cream

STUFF TO DO:

1. Melt the butter in a soup pot on medium heat.
2. Add the onions, green pepper, lemon juice, garlic, salt, and pepper. Sauté for 5 minutes, stirring with a wooden spoon.
3. Add half the cabbage and half the tomatoes, and simmer for 5 minutes, stirring occasionally.
4. Add the remaining cabbage and tomatoes and 5 cups of water, and stir.
5. Bring to a boil, then reduce heat and simmer, covered, for 20 minutes.
6. Ladle into bowls and garnish.

Makes four to six servings

BLUE BAYOU

This cheddar cheese soup is like soup fondue.

STUFF:

1	large potato, peeled and chopped
2	tablespoons butter
1	small leek, chopped
1	tablespoon cooking sherry or dry white wine (optional)
1	clove garlic, pressed, or 1 teaspoon garlic powder
⅛	teaspoon nutmeg
¼	teaspoon salt
½	teaspoon pepper
12	ounces sharp cheddar cheese, grated (3 cups)
2	cups half-and-half

Garnish: blue tortilla chips and grated cheddar cheese

STUFF TO DO:

1. Boil the potato in 3 cups of water until tender, about 15 minutes. Drain, save the broth, and set the potato aside.
2. Melt the butter in a soup pot on medium heat.
3. Add the leek, sherry if using, garlic, nutmeg, salt, and pepper. Sauté for 5 minutes, stirring with a wooden spoon.
4. Add the cooked potato and its broth, and stir.
5. Stir in the cheese until blended.
6. In a blender, blend the soup with the half-and-half until thick and silky smooth.
7. Pour into bowls and garnish.

Makes four to six servings

EXTRA, EXTRA,

★ ★ ★ ★

EAT ALL ABOUT IT!

ANNABANANA BREAD

Good bread is a necessary addition to soup. The two together are one of the great relationships in food.

STUFF:

2	cups sifted all-purpose flour
1	teaspoon baking soda
½	teaspoon salt
½	cup butter or shortening, at room temperature
1	cup sugar
2	eggs
2	bananas, mashed (1 cup)
⅓	cup milk
1	teaspoon fresh lemon juice
½	cup chopped walnuts

STUFF TO DO:

1. Preheat the oven to 350°F.
2. In a mixing bowl, sift the flour with the baking soda and salt.
3. In another bowl, gradually add the sugar to the butter, mixing well.
4. Mix in the eggs and bananas.
5. In a third bowl, mix the milk and lemon juice.
6. In alternating turns, add the flour mixture and the milk mixture to the banana mixture, starting and ending with the flour mixture (flour to banana mix, milk to banana mix, flour to banana mix, milk to banana mix, flour to banana mix).
7. Stir in the nuts.
8. Grease the bottom of a bread pan, and pour in the batter.
9. Bake for 60 to 70 minutes, until the bread springs back when lightly touched in the center.
10. Remove the bread from the pan to a plate and let cool before serving.
    Makes one loaf

MUFFIN BUT THE BEST

Corny is good.

STUFF:

1 cup sifted all-purpose flour
1 cup cornmeal
2 tablespoons sugar
4 teaspoons baking powder
1 teaspoon salt
2 eggs, slightly beaten
1 cup milk
¼ cup vegetable oil

STUFF TO DO:

1. Preheat the oven to 425°F.
2. Line a 12-cup muffin tin with paper liners.
3. In a mixing bowl, sift the flour with the cornmeal, sugar, baking powder, and salt.
4. In another bowl, combine the eggs, milk, and vegetable oil.
5. Make a deep hole in the center of the dry ingredients.
6. Pour the liquid ingredients into the hole.
7. Stir until smooth.
8. Fill muffin cups two-thirds full.
9. Bake for 15 to 20 minutes, or until golden brown on top.
   Makes 12 muffins

TALKING HEADS OF LETTUCE

This salad really rocks!

STUFF:

Salad

1	small head of lettuce of your choice
10	cherry tomatoes
1	small cucumber, sliced
½	yellow bell pepper, sliced
½	red bell pepper, sliced
½	small red onion, sliced
½	small red cabbage, sliced or shredded
½	cup dried garbanzo beans, rinsed, soaked overnight in 4 cups water, then boiled in 4 cups water until soft, about 20 minutes; or 1 cup canned garbanzo beans
1	handful of alfalfa sprouts

Russian Dressing

1	cup mayonnaise
½	cup ketchup
⅛	teaspoon salt
¼	teaspoon pepper
1	teaspoon fresh lemon juice

STUFF TO DO:

1. Wash all the vegetables thoroughly.
2. Tear the lettuce into bite-size pieces, and put into a salad bowl.
3. Arrange the other ingredients on top of the lettuce in a pretty pattern of your choice. Save the sprouts for last.
4. Mix all the dressing ingredients together in a small bowl. Drizzle onto the salad.
   Makes four servings

HOLY GUACAMOLE

Heavenly!

STUFF:

4   ripe (but not mushy) avocados
4   teaspoons fresh lemon juice
2   tablespoons sour cream or plain yogurt
1   teaspoon garlic powder
¼   teaspoon salt
½   teaspoon pepper
2   tablespoons chopped tomatoes
2   teaspoons diced onion

STUFF TO DO:

1. Scoop out the avocado into a small mixing bowl. With a masher or a fork, mash it with the lemon juice, sour cream, garlic powder, salt, and pepper.
2. Stir in the tomatoes and onion.
3. Serve with blue tortilla chips.
   Makes four servings

QUESADILLAS

Whatever will be, will be-a!

STUFF:

4   flour or corn tortillas
8   ounces Monterey Jack, cheddar, or mozzarella cheese, grated (1 cup)
1   8-ounce jar salsa or, if you like, anything from peppers to pepperoni

STUFF TO DO:

1. Place one tortilla in a nonstick skillet on medium heat.
2. Sprinkle with one-half of the cheese and salsa, then put a second tortilla on top.
3. Cook for 2 minutes on each side or until lightly browned and the cheese is melted.
4. Remove from the skillet, and cut into pizza wedges.
5. Serve with sour cream, salsa, or guacamole.
   Makes four servings

MACHO NACHOS

Munch a bunch!

STUFF:

3 handfuls of nacho chips

6 ounces Monterey Jack cheese, grated (1 cup)

1 small tomato, diced (about ½ cup) or ½ cup salsa, or both

STUFF TO DO:

1. Place the chips on a microwaveable plate.
2. Sprinkle the cheese and tomato on top.
3. Microwave until the cheese is melted, about 1 minute.
   OR: Broil on a cookie sheet until the cheese is melted, about 3 minutes.
   Makes four servings

COOL-AS-A-CUCUMBER SPREAD

Yeah!

STUFF:

1 small cucumber, peeled

8 ounces cream cheese at room temperature

½ teaspoon chopped fresh or dried dill

⅛ teaspoon salt

⅛ teaspoon pepper

1 teaspoon fresh lemon juice

   Garnish: alfalfa sprouts and cucumber slices

STUFF TO DO:

1. Grate the cucumber into a colander, then squeeze out the juice with your hands.
2. Place the grated cucumber into a medium-size mixing bowl. With a fork or large spoon, mix in the remaining ingredients.
3. Spread on half slices of your favorite bread, and garnish.
   Makes four servings

CRUSTY CROUTONS

Here's how! (Have an adult help.)

> Use one slice of bread for each serving of croutons.

1. Preheat the oven to 325°F.
2. Cut bread into cubes, and place in a large mixing bowl.
3. Add enough olive oil to moisten all the cubes.
4. Sprinkle with spices of your choice, such as basil, oregano, or garlic. Or sprinkle with the grated cheese of your choice, such as Parmesan or cheddar.
5. Place on a cookie sheet, and bake until golden brown and crisp, about 7 to 10 minutes.

SLIM PICKENS

May be left over, but still a great actor!

You can reheat leftover soup. Some soups can be changed by adding a different garnish or by adding a dollop of sour cream. Try baking some of the soups with croutons and grated cheese on top.

EXAMPLES:

1. Best Buddy Soup can be served the next day with sour cream as a garnish.
2. Squish-Squash Soup can be served baked in individual crocks with croutons and shredded Muenster cheese on top.

INDEX